EASY-TO-LEARN SLOW COOKER RECIPE GUIDE

Game Changing Slow Cooked Family Favourites

Simon Brown

ISBN - 9798356425325

Table of Contents

EXCLUSIVE BONUS

40 Weight Loss Recipes

&

14 Days Meal Plan

Scan the QR-Code and receive
the FREE download:

Welcome to Your Easy-To-Learn Slow Cooker Recipe Guide

Welcome to your easy-to-learn slow cooker recipe guide - the only cookbook that any slow cooker owner needs to use!

This is the perfect cookbook for those of you who just getting started in the world of food and cooking. All you need is a slow cooker and you'll be able to create every recipe in this book. Even if you're an avid cook already, you'll enjoy browsing these recipes and adding your own unique spin to traditional, classic dishes.

Inside this cookbook, you'll learn:

- What a slow cooker is
- Where slow cookers began and how they have developed over the years
- What the different types of slow cookers are and their advantages
- The best foods and dishes to cook in a slow cooker
- The best slow cooker is on the market and which brand to buy from
- How to use a slow cooker
- How to clean your slow cooker properly to maintain it for years
- The key benefits of using a slow cooker

All of this information is followed up with a wide range of different recipes for you to try using your handy slow cooker. You'll find recipes for all meals of the day, including breakfast, lunch, dinner, desserts, and snacks. The whole family can enjoy a delicious range of exciting dishes for years to come!

We've included the nutritional values per serving (including calories, carbs, protein, and fats) for every dish so that you can track your caloric of macronutrient intake more easily. We've also added the total preparation and cooking times so that you can plan your meals around your busy schedule.

So, are you ready to get started? Grab your slow cooker and let's get cooking!

What is a Slow Cooker?

Slow cookers are portable electronic kitchen appliances. They have been well-loved for years and their popularity is only increasing by the year thanks to the convenience and versatility that they offer to the user.

Whether you're an avid cook or you like to spend minimal time in the kitchen, you can enjoy everything that the slow cooker has to offer. They're suitable for everybody!

Slow cookers use gentle heat that slowly warms up batches of food to a simmer. They run for several hours and often have a variety of settings and options for you to choose from so that your dishes are cooked to perfection. Most commonly, slow cookers are used to create liquid-based dishes.

You can leave your slow cookers to do their thing for several hours while you head out to work or go and meet your friends. They can be left to cook and simmer your dishes all day, which is why they are so popular in the modern day when people are living busy lives.

Where Did Slow Cookers Begin and How Have They Developed Over the Years?

Slow cookers first gained popularity in the 1940s when women were starting to work more than they ever had before. Mums were trying to balance their full-time or part-time jobs, looking after the children, and doing the housework. Slow cookers provided busy parents with an easy way to cook delicious and nutritious meals without needing to spend hours in the kitchen.

These handy kitchen appliances enabled people to prepare their evening meal in the morning before work, set the slow cooker to simmer, and leave it for several hours while they were out of the house. When they returned home, their dinner was ready to eat, meaning they could relax after a long day without worrying about cooking.

Despite gaining popularity in the 1940s, the slow cooker didn't achieve global popularity until 30 years later. In the 1970s, the production of slow cookers massively increased, and they became commonplace in many people's homes. In fact, you would have had to search long and hard to find a home that *didn't* contain a slow cooker in the 70s.

These handy electronic devices are still popular to this very day for the same reason. People are always looking to save time and the slow cooker enables families to continue eating healthily while increasing cooking efficiency.

The modern day slow cooker is much more advanced than the original devices that were created in the 1940s. Nowadays, slow cookers come in a range of sizes, shapes, and designs. They have different cooking settings, insertable trays, and self-cleaning mechanisms that make the cooking process quicker and easier than ever before.

What Are the Different Types of Slow Cookers?

Slow cookers are usually made out of metal or ceramic due to the conductibility of these materials. You can also get porcelain options, but these are less popular.

Metal slow cookers are most commonly made out of aluminium and they usually have a non-stick coating, which makes the appliance light and portable. However, additional metals can be used.

Slow cookers have a large, empty vessel where you add all of your ingredients. This vessel is directly above a metal heating unit. When you plug the slow cooker in and turn the machine, the metal heating unit receives an electrical current that causes it to heat up. This heat transfers to the food that is sitting above and causes it to cook over the course of several hours.

There are four main types of slow cookers that you can buy, which we have discussed below.

Manual slow cooker

A manual slow cooker is the most basic form of this electronic device. It has an adjustable knob that enables you to choose different cooking times and intensities. It's suitable for cooking simple dishes with minimal ingredients.

Generally, manual slow cookers have settings that range from 3-4 or 6-8 hours or low to high.

Programmable slow cooker

As the name suggests, a programmable slow cooker comes with a number of pre-programmed settings that you can choose from when you're cooking. You can set the time and temperature yourself.

This type of slow cooker works using an internal heating element and sensors that enable the machine to maintain a specific cooking temperature so that your meal is cooked to perfection.

Multi-functional slow cooker

A multi-functional slow cooker has several compartments that enable you to cook more than one dish at a time. You can set each compartment to a different temperature or time setting so that none of your dishes are undercooked or overcooked. There is a digital panel that has automatic heating functions so you can keep certain compartments warm while you're waiting for the dishes in the other compartments to cook.

Multi-functional slow cookers are the best option to save time, energy, and money, as they are efficient and use less energy than traditional cooking ovens.

Digital slow cookers

Digital slow cookers are some of the most modern and advanced options. You can control them remotely using an app on your phone, meaning you can cook your dishes while you're at work.

Because they have programmable settings, digital slow cookers make cooking as simple and stress-free as possible without compromising on the taste and quality of your dishes.

Simon Brown

What Dishes Can You Make in a Slow Cooker?

You can cook a wide range of dishes that are predominantly liquid based in any type of slow cooker. Some of the most common dishes that people enjoy creating in slow cookers include soups, stews, curries, and casseroles.

However, the list of dishes that you can cook in a slow cooker is endless, and your handy kitchen device can be used to cook meals for breakfast, lunch, dinner, desserts, and snacks.

Popular foods that can be cooked inside a slow cooker include:

1. Tofu, tempeh, and other soy-based meat alternatives
2. Poultry and white meat, including chicken, turkey, and fish
3. Red meat, such as beef, pork, sausages, bacon, duck, and lamb
4. White potatoes, sweet potatoes, parsnips, turnips, swede, carrots, and cauliflower
5. Leafy green vegetables

No matter what your favourite dish is, it's likely that you can use the slow cooker to create it. Be sure to check the timings and settings used in each slow cooker recipe to prevent certain ingredients from becoming too dry during the cooking process.

Great dishes to create using your slow cooker include:

1. Soups
2. Stews
3. Casseroles
4. Curries
5. Chili
6. Dumplings
7. Traditional 'fry up' dishes with sausages, bacon, beans, and hash browns
8. Brownies
9. Cookies
10. Cream-based desserts
11. Cakes
12. Chocolate pudding

You can fry your ingredients before adding them into the slow cooker compartment if you want to add a bit of extra crispiness to your dishes. Alternatively, you can skip the frying pan and place your raw ingredients straight into the device for a softer, mushier texture.

Simon Brown

What Are the Best Slow Cookers on the Market?

You're not short on choice when you want to treat yourself to a slow cooker. There are hundreds of different slow cooker models available from a wide range of brands.

Depending on your needs and preferences, you might benefit from a particular type of slow cooker. It's important to consider what type of slow cooker you want to get out of the four that we have mentioned above so that you can narrow down your decision and find the best option.

Some important factors to keep in mind when shopping for a new slow cooker are:

1. Type
2. Programmable settings
3. Pre-programmed settings
4. Digital controls
5. Removable inserts
6. Number of compartments
7. Brand
8. Design
9. Size

10. Price

11. Customer reviews

12. Lifespan

13. Manufacturer warranty

Here are some of the best brands or stores that offer premium-quality slow cookers:

- Morphy Richards
- Tefal
- Russell Hobbs
- Cookworks
- Daewoo
- John Lewis
- Ninja
- Swan
- Lakeland
- Argos
- Amazon
- Curry's

How Do You Use a Slow Cooker?

Slow cookers are easy to use, even for those of you who aren't very handy in the kitchen. Whether you're a complete beginner at cooking or you're a professional chef, you can enjoy the simplicity and convenience that slow cookers provide.

All you need to do is prepare your ingredients, add them to the slow cooker compartment, plug the machine in, find the perfect setting, and leave the device to do its thing for the day. Once the cooking time has finished, you'll have a ready-to-eat dish that you and your loved ones can enjoy.

If your food is cooked before you're ready to eat, you can switch the slow cooker onto its 'warm' setting, so that your dish doesn't go cold before you serve it.

Even though every slow cooker model varies slightly, the general settings are the same. The buttons and controls are easy to navigate and every manufacturer includes an extensive user manual with their products.

The manual will also contain the details of your product's warranty. If your machine breaks, you may be eligible to get a repair or replacement for free depending on the details of your warranty.

How Do You Look After a Slow Cooker?

Slow cookers are easy to maintain and keep clean. Many have self-cleaning mechanisms so all you need to do is wipe the outside of the machine or clean up any splashes and spillages. They have removable compartments or trays that you can wash in the sink or dishwasher.

How to Clean Your Slow Cooker

It's important to clean your slow cooker after every use. Even if it doesn't look dirty, there could be small spots of food left over after the cooking process. If these food spots are left to dry for several days, they could harden and become very difficult to remove.

When cleaning your slow cooker, make sure to clean every surface, including the exterior, interior compartments, and base of the machine to ensure there are no food spots left untouched.

Here are some key steps to follow when cleaning your slow cooker:

1. Unplug the device and allow it to cool down before you clean it
2. Use a clean microfibre cloth and soak it with warm water along with washing up liquid to clean the outside of your machine

3. Use a toothbrush or a small, bristled brush to clean the small corners and crevices of the machine that are hard to reach with a standard cloth

4. Remove the interior component from your machine and wash it in the sink or dishwasher after every use. This will prevent food from drying inside the tray in between uses

5. Avoid using harsh scrubbing or very abrasive sponges that could damage or scratch the metal components of the machine

6. If there are any stubborn spots of dried food on your slow cooker, use a combination of baking soda or vinegar with warm water, and apply it to the stains using a microfibre cloth

What Are the Benefits of Using a Slow Cooker?

The benefits of using a slow cooker are endless. Below, we have discussed some of the key benefits and why you should consider investing in this handy kitchen gadget.

1. Slow cookers are easy to use, even for beginners
2. You can cook several dishes at once using a multi-functional slow cooker
3. Slow cookers provide a relatively mess-free method of cooking
4. Slow cookers can be left for several hours without intervention
5. Digital slow cookers can be controlled remotely so you can cook while you're out of the house
6. Slow cookers are energy efficient so you can save on your utility bills and cut your carbon footprint
7. You can enjoy a wide variety of dishes using a slow cooker
8. If you're trying to cook healthier meals, the slow cooker enables you to do so with ease

You can cut your food wastage by creating multiple dishes using the same ingredients

1. Slow cookers come in a wide variety of designs and styles

2. Many slow cookers are small enough to store in your cupboards so you can keep your kitchen countertop clear

EXCLUSIVE BONUS

40 Weight Loss Recipes

&

14 Days Meal Plan

Scan the QR-Code and receive
the FREE download:

Recipes

Now you've learned everything you need to know about slow cookers, it's time to start creating your very own delicious dishes at home. Below, you will find recipes covering all mealtimes, including breakfast, lunch, dinner, and snacks. You can enjoy these dishes by yourself or with your friends and family members.

Breakfast

If you're using your slow cooker to prepare breakfast, you'll need to organize your ingredients and switch your device on the night before so that your dish is ready when you wake up. We haven't included this step in any of the recipes below, but this is something that you'll need to do for every single breakfast dish in this cookbook if you want to enjoy your meal shortly after you wake up.

Most dishes take at least 3-4 hours in the slow cooker, but some require 7-8 hours of cooking time. Unless you want to wake up several hours before you eat, it's best to prepare your dish in the evening and allow your breakfast to cook while you're sleeping.

Slow Cooker All-Day Breakfast

MAKES 2 SERVINGS

PREPARATION TIME – 10 MINUTES

COOKING TIME – 8 HOURS

NUTRITIONAL VALUE PER SERVING – 659 KCALS, 41 G CARBS, 43 G PROTEIN, 40 G FAT

Ingredients

◈ 4 sausages

◈ 8 rashers of bacon

◈ 1 x 400g / 14 oz can of chopped tomatoes

◈ 1 x 400g / 14 oz baked beans

◈ 4 eggs, beaten

◈ 200g button mushrooms

◈ 2 tsp butter

Method

1. Coat the inner compartment of the slow cooker with olive oil or cover it with greaseproof paper.
2. Place the sausages and bacon around the edges of the slow cooker compartment, making sure they aren't stuck together or touching.
3. Add the remaining ingredients to the slow cooker and give everything a good stir.
4. Switch the slow cooker onto a low heat setting, close the lid, and allow it to cook for 8 hours.
5. Once all of the ingredients are cooked, turn the slow cooker off and serve your all-day breakfast with a coffee or glass of fruit juice.

Slow Cooker Peanut Butter Oatmeal

MAKES 4 SERVINGS

PREPARATION TIME – 5 MINUTES

COOKING TIME – 8 HOURS

NUTRITIONAL VALUE PER SERVING – 212 KCALS, 30 G CARBS, 10 G PROTEIN, 6 G FAT

Ingredients

◈ 200 g / 7 oz classic rolled oats

◈ 50 0ml water

◈ 500 ml oat milk

◈ 2 tbsp smooth peanut butter

◈ 2 tbsp chia seeds

Method

1. Cover the inner compartment of the slow cooker with greaseproof paper.
2. In a bowl, add the rolled oats, water, oat milk, peanut butter, and chia seeds. Stir until they form a smooth and consistent mixture.
3. Transfer the mixture to the slow cooker compartment, shut the lid, and cook on a low heat setting for 7-8 hours.
4. In the morning, serve your oatmeal with a topping of your choice. You might want some fresh banana and strawberry slices, a sprinkle of cinnamon, or an extra dollop of peanut butter.

Easy 5-Ingredients Slow Cooker Granola

MAKES 8 SERVINGS

PREPARATION TIME – 10 MINUTES

COOKING TIME – 3 HOURS

NUTRITIONAL VALUE PER SERVING – 145 KCALS, 28 G CARBS, 9 G PROTEIN, 5 G FAT

Ingredients

❖ 200 g / 7 oz old-fashioned oats

❖ 50 g / 1.8 oz brown rice cereal

❖ 2 egg whites

❖ 2 tbsp agave syrup or honey

❖ 2 tbsp mixed seeds (pumpkin, sunflower, and chia seeds)

Method

1. Coat the inner compartment of the slow cooker with olive oil or cover it with greaseproof paper.
2. In a mixing bowl, combine the oats and rice cereal.
3. In a separate bowl, whisk together the egg whites and agave syrup or honey.
4. Mix the wet mixture into the cereal mixture until well-combined. Stir in the mixed seeds.
5. Transfer the cereal mixture to the lined compartment of the slow cooker and close the lid.
6. Cook for 2 and a half hours on a high heat setting until the oats and cereal are lovely and crispy. Lift the lid and stir the granola around to prevent it from burning. Close the lid and cook for a further 30 minutes.
7. Serve the granola with some Greek yoghurt and fresh fruit. Store any leftovers in an airtight jar.

Overnight Protein Oats (Proats)

MAKES 8 SERVINGS

PREPARATION TIME – 10 MINUTES

COOKING TIME – 8 HOURS

NUTRITIONAL VALUE PER SERVING – 234 KCALS, 40 G CARBS, 15 G PROTEIN, 6 G FAT

Ingredients

◈ 100 g / 3.5 oz rolled oats

◈ 500 ml almond or oat milk

◈ 300 ml water (or however much is needed)

◈ 1 scoop protein powder (any flavour)

Method

1. Use greaseproof paper to coat the inner compartment of the slow cooker.
2. Mix the rolled oats, almond or oat milk, water, and protein powder of your choice in a bowl until they form a smooth and consistent mixture. You might need to add more or less water depending on how thick or watery you like your oats. Note that the oats will absorb excess water during the cooking process.
3. Transfer the mixture to the slow cooker compartment, shut the lid, and cook on a low heat setting for 7-8 hours or on a high heat setting for 3-4 hours.
4. Serve your proats with toppings of your choice when you wake up. It's a great pre-workout snack to fuel your body with carbohydrates and protein.

Berry and Banana Granola

MAKES 8 SERVINGS

PREPARATION TIME – 5 MINUTES

COOKING TIME – 2-3 HOURS

NUTRITIONAL VALUE PER SERVING – 154 KCALS, 18 G CARBS, 8 G PROTEIN, 5 G FAT

Ingredients

◈ 100 g / 3.5 oz raw and unsalted mixed nuts (peanuts, cashews, and walnuts)

◈ 100 g / 3.5 oz raw and unsalted mixed seeds (pumpkin, sunflower, and chia)

◈ 100 g / 3.5 oz dried berries

◈ 100 g / 3.5 oz dried banana chips, chopped into small pieces

◈ 400 g / 14 oz rolled oats

◈ 100 g / 7 oz unsweetened coconut flakes

◈ 2 tsp cinnamon

◈ 1 tsp nutmeg

◈ 2 tbsp coconut oil or olive oil

◈ 4 tbsp honey or agave syrup

◈ 1 tbsp vanilla extract

Method

1. Cover the inner component of your slow cooker with parchment paper.

2. In a large mixing bowl, combine the mixed nuts, mixed seeds, dried berries, dried banana chips, rolled oats, coconut flakes, cinnamon, and nutmeg. Mix well.

3. Add the coconut oil or olive oil, honey or agave syrup, and vanilla extract. Toss to coat all of the ingredients until they begin to form small clumps.

4. Transfer the mixture to the slow cooker and close the lid. Turn the slow cooker onto a high heat and cook for 2-3 hours until the granola is golden and crispy. Stir the mixture every 15-30 minutes while it's cooking inside the machine.

5. Serve the granola for breakfast on top of some yogurt or with some milk. Store any leftovers in an airtight jar for a maximum of 5 days.

Delicious Slow Cooker Bread

MAKES 8 SERVINGS

PREPARATION TIME – 15 MINUTES

COOKING TIME – 2 HOURS

NUTRITIONAL VALUE PER SERVING – 167 KCALS, 31 G CARBS, 15 G PROTEIN, 3 G FAT

Ingredients

◈ 400 g / 14 oz wholemeal flour or white flour, or a mixture of both

◈ 1 x 7 g sachet of fast-action dried yeast

◈ 1 tsp sea salt

◈ 400 ml warm water

Method

1. Grease the inner component of your slow cooker with some butter or olive oil, or line it with parchment paper.
2. In a large mixing bowl, combine the flour, yeast, and salt. Stir well.
3. Make a well in the middle and pour 400 ml of warm water into the well. Mix well to form a sticky dough. Add more water or flour if needed to achieve a dough-like consistency.
4. Roll the dough onto a lightly floured surface and knead for 10 minutes until it becomes smooth and elastic.
5. Shape the dough into a large, tight ball and transfer it to the slow cooker. Close the lid and cook on high for 2 hours until the crust is golden and crispy.
6. Remove the dough and cut it into slices. Enjoy with your favourite toppings

Slow Cooker Egg, Cheese, and Ham Casserole

MAKES 4 SERVINGS

PREPARATION TIME – 10 MINUTES

COOKING TIME – 8 HOURS

NUTRITIONAL VALUE PER SERVING – 498 KCALS, 17 G CARBS, 30 G PROTEIN, 36 G FAT

Ingredients

◈ 8 eggs, beaten

◈ 200 ml milk

◈ 1 tsp salt

◈ 1 tsp black pepper

◈ 200 g / 7 oz smoked ham, pre-cooked and chopped

◈ 50g / 1.8 oz cheddar cheese, grated

Method

1. Coat the inner compartment of the slow cooker with olive oil or cover it with greaseproof paper.
2. In a large mixing bowl, whisk together the eggs, milk, salt, and black pepper until well-combined.
3. Stir in half of the precooked smoked ham and transfer the mixture into the slow cooker. Sprinkle the remaining ham and cheddar cheese over the top.
4. Close the lid and cook on a low heat setting for 8 hours.
5. Serve the casserole while hot for breakfast.

Simon Brown

Oat and Raisin Muffins

MAKES 8 SERVINGS

PREPARATION TIME – 15 MINUTES

COOKING TIME – 6 HOURS

NUTRITIONAL VALUE PER SERVING – 213 KCALS, 25 G CARBS, 15 G PROTEIN, 11 G FAT

Ingredients

◈ 200 g / 7 oz rolled oats

◈ 200 g / 7 oz plain flour

◈ 2 tsp baking powder

◈ 100 g / 3.5 oz caster sugar

◈ 100 g / 3.5 oz raisins

◈ 1 egg, beaten

◈ 200 ml milk (any type)

◈ ½ tsp vanilla extract

◈ 1 tbsp chia seeds

Method

1. Grease an 8-pan muffin tray with olive oil.
2. In a bowl, combine the rolled oats, plain flour, baking powder, and caster sugar until it fully mixed. Stir in the raisins.
3. In a separate bowl, combine the beaten egg, milk, and vanilla extract.
4. Pour the wet mixture into the dry mixture and whisk until fully combined into one smooth mixture. Add the chia seeds and stir well.
5. Spoon the mixture evenly into the 8 compartments of the muffin tray.
6. Carefully transfer the muffin tray into the slow cooker and close the lid.
7. Cook the muffins on a low setting for 6 hours.
8. Once cooked, the top of the muffins should be golden and the inside should be relatively dry. You can test this by inserting a knife into the centre of the muffins. It should come out dry when the muffins are fully cooked.
9. Serve the muffins hot or cold. Store any leftovers in an airtight loaf tin and consume within 5-7 days.

Simon Brown

Breakfast Banana Bread

MAKES 8 SERVINGS

PREPARATION TIME – 15 MINUTES

COOKING TIME – 6 HOURS

NUTRITIONAL VALUE PER SERVING – 178 KCALS, 21 G CARBS, 10 G PROTEIN, 8 G FAT

Ingredients

◈ 4 ripe bananas, and an extra ½ for toppings

◈ 400 ml milk (any type)

◈ 1 egg, beaten

◈ 200 g / 7 oz plain flour

◈ 200 g / 7 oz wholemeal flour

◈ 2 tsp baking powder

◈ 2 tbsp brown sugar

◈ 1 tsp vanilla extract

◈ 1 tsp nutmeg

Method

1. Grease a loaf tin with olive oil.
2. Place the bananas into a large mixing bowl and mash well.
3. In a separate bowl, whisk together the milk and egg. Set aside.
4. In a third bowl, combine the plain flour, wholemeal flour, baking powder, and brown sugar.
5. Pour the milk and egg mixture into the mashed bananas and mix well. Stir in the vanilla extract and a sprinkle of nutmeg.
6. Fold the dry ingredients into the wet mixture and stir well until a smooth dough has formed.
7. Pour the mixture into the prepared loaf tin and transfer to the slow cooker.
8. Close the lid and turn the slow cooker onto a low heat setting. Cook for 6-8 hours until the banana bread is golden and firm on the top. Insert a knife into the centre of the loaf to check that it is cooked all the way through. The knife should come out dry when the loaf is ready.
9. Serve the banana bread hot or cold for breakfast.

Lunch

Your slow cooker can also be used to create delicious lunch dishes too! Give the recipes below a go when you've got a day at home and want to make something more exciting than a sandwich!

Fresh Tomato Soup

MAKES 8 SERVINGS

PREPARATION TIME – 15 MINUTES

COOKING TIME – 2 HOURS

NUTRITIONAL VALUE PER SERVING – 167 KCALS, 15 G CARBS, 6 G PROTEIN, 7 G FAT

Ingredients

◈ 1 tbsp olive oil

◈ 1 white onion, chopped

◈ 1 clove garlic, peeled and crushed

◈ 1 red pepper, sliced

◈ 200g fresh beef tomatoes, quartered

◈ 1 x 400g / 14 oz can of chopped tomatoes

◈ 1 tsp brown sugar

◈ 1 tsp black pepper

◈ 1 tsp dried chives

Method

1. Coat the inner compartment of the slow cooker with olive oil or cover it with greaseproof paper.
2. Heat 1 tbsp olive oil in a frying pan.
3. Add the onions and garlic, and cook over medium heat for 8-10 until the onions have softened and caramelised.
4. Transfer the onions and garlic to the slow cooker and add the rest of the soup ingredients. Close the lid and cook on a high heat for 2 hours.
5. Transfer the hot soup to a blender or food processor. Pulse the soup in 30 second intervals until smooth and consistent.
6. Serve the soup while steaming hot with a side of crusty bread.

Slow Cooker Wholemeal Burritos

MAKES 8 SERVINGS

PREPARATION TIME – 20 MINUTES

COOKING TIME – 4 HOURS

NUTRITIONAL VALUE PER SERVING – 514 KCALS, 38 G CARBS, 27 G PROTEIN, 14 G FAT

Ingredients

- 2 x vegetable stock cubes
- 200 g / 7 oz brown rice, dry and uncooked
- 1 x 400 g / 14 oz can kidney beans
- 1 x 400 g / 14 oz can black beans
- 1 x 400 g / 14 oz chopped tomatoes
- 1 white onion, finely sliced
- ½ red pepper, finely sliced
- ½ yellow pepper, finely sliced
- 1 tsp chili powder
- 1 tsp cayenne pepper
- 1 tbsp cheddar cheese, grated
- 4 wholemeal tortillas

Method

1. Cover the inner compartment of the slow cooker with greaseproof paper.
2. Dissolve the stock cubes in boiling water according to the packet instructions. Pour the stock into the slow cooker compartment.
3. In a large mixing bowl, combine the brown rice, kidney beans, black beans, chopped tomatoes, white onion, red pepper, and yellow pepper. Stir to mix well.
4. Sprinkle 1 tsp each of chili powder and cayenne pepper into the mixture and stir.
5. Lay out the wholemeal tortillas on a flat surface and spoon the burrito mixture evenly into the centre of each. Top each with grated cheddar cheese.
6. Carefully roll up the burritos and use cocktail sticks to secure them and ensure the ingredients don't spill out during the cooking process.
7. Transfer the burritos to the prepared slow cooker component and close the lid.
8. Turn the slow cooker onto a low heat setting and cook the burritos for at least 4 hours. The burritos should be hot and crispy on the outside.
9. Serve the burritos while steaming hot with an extra sprinkle of cheddar cheese and a side of salsa and guacamole.

Sticky Tofu and Noodles

MAKES 4 SERVINGS

PREPARATION TIME – 10 MINUTES

COOKING TIME – 4 HOURS

NUTRITIONAL VALUE PER SERVING – 315 KCALS, 28 G CARBS, 30 G PROTEIN, 13 G FAT

Ingredients

- 1 x 400 g / 14 oz block firm tofu, diced
- 1 tbsp soy sauce
- 1 tsp honey
- 1 tsp white vinegar
- 1 tbsp olive oil
- 1 white onion, finely sliced
- 2 x vegetable stock cubes
- 2 carrots, peeled and chopped
- 100 g / 3.5 oz baby sweetcorn
- 100 g / 3.5 oz carrots, sliced
- 4 nests of white or wholemeal noodles
- 1 tsp black pepper

Method

1. Coat the inner compartment of the slow cooker with olive oil or cover it with greaseproof paper.
2. Place the diced tofu in a bowl. In a separate small mixing bowl, combine the soy sauce, honey, and white vinegar.
3. Toss the tofu in the sauce until fully coated and set aside.
4. Heat the olive oil in a frying pan and cook the onion over medium heat for 8-10 minutes until softened.
5. Dissolve the vegetable stock cubes in boiling water according to the packet instructions and pour this into the prepared slow cooker compartment.
6. Add the coated tofu, onion, carrots, baby sweetcorn, and carrots to the slow cooker. Close the lid and cook for 4 hours on a medium to high setting.
7. Just before the tofu mixture is cooked, place a pan of water over high heat and bring it to a boil.
8. Lower the heat to a simmer and add the noodles. Cook for 10-12 minutes until the noodles are soft and fully cooked.
9. Split the noodles into four even portions in separate bowls.
10. Serve the tofu mixture on top of each bed of noodles while still hot.

Slow Cooker Creamy Carrot Soup

MAKES 8 SERVINGS

PREPARATION TIME – 15 MINUTES

COOKING TIME – 8 HOURS

NUTRITIONAL VALUE PER SERVING – 134 KCALS, 13 G CARBS, 5 G PROTEIN, 2 G FAT

Ingredients

◈ 1 tbsp olive oil

◈ 1 white onion, finely chopped

◈ 2 carrots, peeled and thinly sliced

◈ 2 x vegetable stock cubes

◈ 100 ml single cream

◈ 1 tsp black pepper

Method

1. Cover the inner compartment of the slow cooker with olive oil or greaseproof paper.

2. Heat the olive oil in a frying pan and cook the onion for 8-10 minutes until it is soft and fragrant. Add the carrots and cook for a further 4-5 minutes.

3. Add the onions and carrots to the prepared slow cooker compartment, followed by the vegetable stock cubes, single cream, black pepper, and around 300ml of water.

4. Close the lid and turn the slow cooker to a low heat setting. Cook the soup for 8 hours until hot and smooth.

5. Once cooked, transfer the soup to a blender and pulse in 30 second intervals until smooth and creamy.

6. Serve piping hot with a side of bread and butter.

Slow Cooker Chicken and Veggie Casserole

MAKES 4 SERVINGS

PREPARATION TIME – 15 MINUTES

COOKING TIME – 8 HOURS

NUTRITIONAL VALUE PER SERVING – 368 KCALS, 34 G CARBS, 31 G PROTEIN, 18 G FAT

Ingredients

- 400 g / 14 oz chicken breast, pre-cooked and diced
- 1 white onion, finely sliced
- ½ red pepper, finely sliced
- 1 carrot, finely sliced
- 1 stick celery, finely sliced
- 4 eggs, beaten
- 200 ml milk (any type)
- 2 tbsp plain flour
- 1 tsp salt
- ½ tsp black pepper
- 30g cheddar cheese, grated

Method

1. Cover the inner compartment of the slow cooker with olive oil or greaseproof paper.
2. Add the chicken breast, white onion, red pepper, carrot, and celery to the lined slow cooker insert.
3. In a bowl, whisk together the eggs, milk, flour, salt, and black pepper. Pour this mixture into the slow cooker, fully covering the chicken and vegetables.
4. Turn the slow cooker onto a low to medium heat setting, close the lid, and cook the casserole for 8 hours.
5. Around 10 minutes before the casserole is due to be fully cooked, open the lid and sprinkle the grated cheddar cheese evenly across the top.
6. Close the lid once again and allow the casserole to continue cooking until the full 8 hours is up.
7. Serve the casserole with some dumplings or noodles.

Crispy Chicken Noodle Soup

MAKES 4 SERVINGS

PREPARATION TIME – 15 MINUTES

COOKING TIME – 8 HOURS

NUTRITIONAL VALUE PER SERVING – 423 KCALS, 29 G CARBS, 31 G PROTEIN, 7 G FAT

Ingredients

- ❖ 2 x chicken stock cubes
- ❖ 400 g / 14 oz boneless, skinless chicken breast, diced
- ❖ 1 white onion, finely sliced
- ❖ 1 clove garlic, peeled and crushed
- ❖ 2 carrots, peeled and finely sliced
- ❖ 1 leek, finely chopped
- ❖ 50 g / 1.8 oz mange tout
- ❖ 1 tsp salt
- ❖ 1 tsp black pepper
- ❖ 4 nests of dry white noodles

Method

1. Cover the inner compartment of the slow cooker with olive oil or greaseproof paper.

2. Dissolve the chicken stock cubes in the required amount of boiling water as per the packet and pour into the prepared slow cooker compartment.

3. In a large bowl, add the chicken breast, white onion, garlic clove, carrots, leek, mange tout, salt, and black pepper. Combine well and transfer to the slow cooker.

4. Close the lid and switch the slow cooker machine onto a low heat setting. Cook for 8 hours until the chicken is well-cooked, and the vegetables are soft.

5. Just before the slow cooker ingredients are due to come out of the machine, place a pan of water over high heat and bring it to a boil.

6. Lower the heat to a simmer and add the noodles. Cook for 10-12 minutes until the noodles are soft and fully cooked.

7. Separate the noodles into four bowls and pour the chicken broth mixture on top. Serve while hot.

Cheese and Ham Slow Cooker Omelette

MAKES 4 SERVINGS

PREPARATION TIME – 10 MINUTES

COOKING TIME – 1 HOUR

NUTRITIONAL VALUE PER SERVING – 188 KCALS, 10 G CARBS, 12 G PROTEIN, 11 G FAT

Ingredients

◈ 8 eggs, beaten

◈ 100 ml milk (any type)

◈ 50 g / 1.8 oz cheddar cheese, grated

◈ 50 g / 1.8 oz smoked ham, chopped into small pieces

◈ 1 tsp dried herbs

◈ 1 tsp black pepper

Method

1. Cover the inner compartment of the slow cooker with olive oil or greaseproof paper.
2. In a bowl, whisk together the eggs and milk. Stir in the cheddar cheese and chopped ham.
3. Sprinkle some dried herbs ad black pepper into the mixture.
4. Transfer to the prepared slow cooker compartment and close the lid. Turn onto a high heat setting and cook until the eggs are fully cooked.
5. Serve the cheese and ham omelette while hot with a sprinkle of extra cheese and a side salad.

Spicy Tempeh, Potatoes, and Veggies

MAKES 8 SERVINGS

PREPARATION TIME – 20 MINUTES

COOKING TIME – 6 HOURS

NUTRITIONAL VALUE PER SERVING – 342 KCALS, 20 G CARBS, 29 G PROTEIN, 12 G FAT

Ingredients

- 2 x vegetable stock cubes
- 1 tbsp olive oil
- 1 white onion, finely chopped
- 1 green pepper, finely sliced
- 1 white potato, peeled and diced
- 1 x 400 g / 14 oz block tempeh, diced
- 1 courgette, diced
- 1 tsp chili powder
- 1 tsp cayenne pepper
- 1 tsp paprika

Method

1. Coat the inner compartment of the slow cooker with olive oil or cover it with greaseproof paper.
2. Dissolve the vegetable stock cubes in the required amount of boiling water as per the packet and pour into the prepared slow cooker compartment.
3. Heat the olive oil in a frying pan and cook the onion, pepper, and potato slices for 8-10 minutes until they are all slightly soft.
4. Transfer the vegetables to the slow cooker, followed by the tempeh and courgette. Sprinkle 1 tsp each of chili powder, cayenne pepper, and paprika into the mixture.
5. Close the slow cooker lid and switch it onto a low heat setting. Cook the tempeh and vegetables for 6 hours until fully cooked.
6. Serve while hot.

Slow Cooker BBQ Lentils

MAKES 4 SERVINGS

PREPARATION TIME – 10 MINUTES

COOKING TIME – 8 HOURS

NUTRITIONAL VALUE PER SERVING – 283 KCALS, 30 G CARBS, 19 G PROTEIN, 8 G FAT

Ingredients

- ❖ 200 g / 7 oz dry red lentils
- ❖ 1 clove garlic, peeled and crushed
- ❖ 1 tbsp dried cumin
- ❖ 1 x 400 g / 14 oz can of chopped tomatoes
- ❖ 4 tbsp BBQ sauce
- ❖ 400 ml water

Method

1. Coat the inner compartment of the slow cooker with olive oil or cover it with greaseproof paper.

2. Add all of the ingredients to a mixing bowl and stir well until fully combined.

3. Transfer to the slow cooker, shut the lid, and cook on a low heat setting for 8 hours until the lentils have fully absorbed the water and are soft.

4. Keep checking the mixture every hour or two and add more water if required to prevent the lentils from becoming too dry.

5. Serve the lentils with a sprinkle of black pepper and an extra squirt of BBQ sauce.

Slow Cooker Chicken and Veggie Pasta

MAKES 4 SERVINGS

PREPARATION TIME – 15 MINUTES

COOKING TIME – 4 HOURS

NUTRITIONAL VALUE PER SERVING – 332 KCALS, 34 G CARBS, 25 G PROTEIN, 5 G FAT

Ingredients

◈ 400 g / 14 oz boneless chicken breast, pre-cooked and sliced

◈ 1 onion, sliced

◈ 1 stick celery, sliced

◈ 1 carrot, chopped

◈ 1 tsp dried mixed herbs

◈ 1 tsp black pepper

◈ 1 x 400 g / 14 oz pasta, dry and uncooked

◈ 1 tsp salt

Simon Brown

Method

1. Coat the inner compartment of the slow cooker with olive oil or cover it with greaseproof paper.
2. Place the chicken, onion, celery, carrot, dried mixed herbs, and black pepper in the slow cooker. Stir well.
3. Close the slow cooker lid and turn it onto a low heat setting. Cook the chicken and vegetables for 4 hours.
4. Just before the slow cooker is due to finish, bring a pan of water to boil and add the pasta. Once boiling, lower the heat to a gentle simmer and add a sprinkle of salt to the pan.
5. Cook the pasta for 10-12 minutes until soft.
6. Split the pasta evenly between 4 dishes and serve with the chicken and vegetable mixture on top.

Dinner

If you're searching for some new and exciting dishes to cook for dinner, your slow cooker will come to the rescue! Below, we've got a wide range of delicious meat-based and meat-free dishes that you can cook for dinner using your slow cooker.

Hot Sauce Chicken Wings

MAKES 4 SERVINGS

PREPARATION TIME – 5 MINUTES

COOKING TIME – 6 HOURS

NUTRITIONAL VALUE PER SERVING – 318 KCALS, 16 G CARBS, 24 G PROTEIN, 13 G FAT

Ingredients

◈ 3 tsp hot sauce

◈ 2 tbsp soy sauce

◈ 3 tbsp honey

◈ Zest 1 lemon

◈ 4 x 100 g / 3.5 oz chicken
   wings

◈ 4 tbsp corn starch

◈ 1 tbsp sesame seeds

◈ 1 tbsp dried chives

◈ 1 tsp black pepper

Method

1. Coat the inner compartment of the slow cooker with olive oil or cover it with greaseproof paper.
2. In a bowl, whisk together the hot sauce, soy sauce, honey, and lemon zest.
3. Take each of the chicken wings one at a time, and gently roll in the sauce to coat on all sides.
4. Transfer the chicken wings to the prepared tray of the slow cooker, making sure they aren't touching each other, and close the lid.
5. Cook the wings on a low to medium heat setting for 6 hours until they are fully cooked and crispy.
6. In a bowl, mix 4 tbsp corn starch with 1 tbsp water and stir well to form a smooth mixture. Stir in the sesame seeds, dried chives, and black pepper.
7. Remove the chicken wings from the slow cooker and coat in the cornstarch mixture. Place back into the slow cooker and cook for a further 10 minutes.
8. Serve the chicken wings with a side of your choice and an extra drizzle of hot sauce.

Chicken Tikka Masala

MAKES 4 SERVINGS

PREPARATION TIME – 20 MINUTES

COOKING TIME – 4 HOURS

NUTRITIONAL VALUE PER SERVING – 452 KCALS, 31 G CARBS, 36 G PROTEIN, 15 G FAT

Ingredients

- ❖ 1 tbsp olive oil
- ❖ 1 tsp cumin seeds
- ❖ 1 tbsp garam masala
- ❖ 1 tbsp curry powder
- ❖ 1 tsp black pepper
- ❖ 1 white onion, finely sliced
- ❖ 2 cloves garlic, peeled and crushed
- ❖ 1 red pepper, finely sliced
- ❖ 1 red chili pepper, finely sliced
- ❖ 2 tbsp tomato paste

- ❖ 1 x 400g can of chopped tomatoes
- ❖ 1 x 400 g / 14 oz boneless, skinless chicken breast, diced
- ❖ 1 tbsp dried coriander

Method

1. Heat 1 tbsp olive oil in a large wok or frying pan and add the cumin seeds.
2. Cook for 1-2 minutes before adding the garam masala, curry powder, and black pepper to the pan. Cook for a further 2 minutes until you can begin to smell the spices.
3. Add the white onion, garlic, red pepper, chili pepper, and tomato paste to the frying pan, and cook for a further 2 minutes.
4. Coat the inner compartment of the slow cooker with olive oil or cover it with greaseproof paper.
5. Transfer the ingredients from the pan to the lined slow cooker tray, pour the chopped tomatoes in, and give it a stir.
6. Add the diced chicken breast and 1 tbsp dried coriander.
7. Close the lid of the slow cooker and turn it to a medium heat setting. Cook the chicken tikka masala for 4 hours until the ingredients are well-cooked, and the dish is hot.
8. Serve with a side of pilau rice, poppadoms, naan bread, and mango chutney.

Slow Cooker Salmon with Creamy Lemon Sauce

MAKES 4 SERVINGS

PREPARATION TIME – 10 MINUTES

COOKING TIME – 3 HOURS

NUTRITIONAL VALUE PER SERVING – 172 KCALS, 8 G CARBS, 29 G PROTEIN, 3 G FAT

Ingredients

For the fish:

- ❖ 3 lemons, sliced
- ❖ 4 x 100 g / 3.5 oz skin-on salmon fillets
- ❖ 1 tbsp olive oil
- ❖ 1 tsp salt
- ❖ 1 tsp black pepper
- ❖ ½ tsp paprika
- ❖ ½ tsp chili powder
- ❖ 1 tsp garlic powder
- ❖ 1 tsp Italian seasoning

For the creamy lemon sauce:

- ❖ 3 tbsp lemon juice
- ❖ 4 tbsp heavy cream
- ❖ 1 tsp fresh parsley, chopped

Method

1. Coat the inner compartment of the slow cooker with olive oil or cover it with greaseproof paper.
2. Arrange the lemon slices along the bottom of the slow cooker.
3. Place the salmon fillets on top of the lemon slices and lightly coat them with olive oil.
4. Evenly sprinkle the salt, black pepper, paprika, chili powder, garlic powder, and Italian seasoning over the top of each salmon fillet. Use your fingers to press the seasoning lightly into the fish.
5. Close the lid of the slow cooker and cook the fish for 2 hours until opaque and flaky. Once cooked, remove the fish from the slow cooker and set aside.
6. To make the creamy lemon sauce, place all of the ingredients in a saucepan and gently heat to a simmer.
7. Heat through for 5-7 minutes.
8. Serve the salmon fillets with the creamy lemon sauce over the top.

Fish Tacos

MAKES 4 SERVINGS

PREPARATION TIME – 10 MINUTES

COOKING TIME – 4-5 HOURS

NUTRITIONAL VALUE PER SERVING – 223 KCALS, 21 G CARBS, 24 G PROTEIN, 12 G FAT

Ingredients

◈ 1 x 400 g / 14 oz can of chopped tomatoes

◈ 1 tbsp chipotle sauce

◈ 1 tbsp fish sauce

◈ 1 tsp salt

◈ 1 tsp black pepper

◈ 2 cloves garlic, peeled and minced

◈ 1 white onion, thinly sliced

◈ 1 x 400 g / 14 oz white fish, flaked

◈ 4 taco shells

Method

1. Cover the inner compartment of the slow cooker with greaseproof paper.
2. In a large mixing bowl, combine the chopped tomatoes, chipotle sauce, fish sauce, salt, and black pepper.
3. Add the garlic, white onion, and flaked fish into the bowl. Stir well to form a consistent mixture.
4. Transfer the mixture to the slow cooker, close the lid, and turn to a medium heat setting. Cook for 4 hours before checking the fish. If it is still slightly undercooked, return to the slow cooker for a further 30-60 minutes until the fish is cooked but not overly dry.
5. Serve the fish mixture evenly into 4 taco shells and top with grated cheddar cheese, sour cream, chunky salsa, and guacamole.

Slow Cooker Beef Bourguignon

MAKES 4 SERVINGS

PREPARATION TIME – 10 MINUTES

COOKING TIME – 8 HOURS

NUTRITIONAL VALUE PER SERVING – 312 KCALS, 20 G CARBS, 28 G PROTEIN, 16 G FAT

Ingredients

- ❖ 1 tbsp olive oil
- ❖ 400 g / 14 oz casserole steak, cut into chunks
- ❖ 8 rashers streaky bacon, chopped
- ❖ 1 white onion, peeled and chopped
- ❖ 2 cloves garlic, peeled and chopped
- ❖ 10 carrots, peeled and chopped
- ❖ 300 ml red wine
- ❖ 2 x beef stock cubes

- ❖ 2 sprigs thyme, finely chopped
- ❖ 1 tsp salt
- ❖ 1 tsp black pepper

Method

1. Coat the inner compartment of the slow cooker with olive oil or cover it with greaseproof paper.
2. Heat half of the oil in a large frying pan and add the steak chunks. Cook for 8-10 minutes until the meat is browned on all sides.
3. Transfer the steak to the slow cooker
4. Add remaining olive oil to the frying pan, followed by the bacon rashers and white onion.
5. Cook for 3-4 minutes before adding the garlic and carrots and cooking for another 4 minutes. At this point, the onions and garlic should be fragrant and softened.
6. Transfer the bacon and vegetables to the slow cooker. Pour the red wine into the slow cooker.
7. Boil a kettle of water and use it to dissolve the beef stock cubes. Add to the slow cooker along with the chopped thyme.
8. Stir the mixture inside the slow cooker compartment and a sprinkle each of salt and black pepper.
9. Close the slow cooker lid and cook for 8 hours.
10. Serve the beef bourguignon with a side of potatoes and vegetables.

Simon Brown

Slow Cooker Chili Con Carne or Non Carne

MAKES 4 SERVINGS

PREPARATION TIME – 15 MINUTES

COOKING TIME – 8 HOURS

NUTRITIONAL VALUE PER SERVING – 411 KCALS, 27G CARBS, 30G PROTEIN, 19G FAT

Ingredients

- ❖ 3 tbsp olive oil
- ❖ 400 g / 14 oz beef mince or soy mince
- ❖ 1 white onion, finely chopped
- ❖ 1 red pepper, sliced
- ❖ 2 cloves garlic, peeled and finely grated
- ❖ 2 tsp chili powder
- ❖ 2 tsp ground cumin
- ❖ 2 tsp smoked paprika
- ❖ 2 tsp dried mixed herbs
- ❖ 1 tsp salt
- ❖ 1 tsp black pepper
- ❖ 4 tbsp tomato purée
- ❖ 1 x 400 g /14 oz can of chopped tomatoes
- ❖ 4 x beef stock cubes or vegetable stock cubes
- ❖ 1 x 400 g / 14 oz can black beans, drained and rinsed
- ❖ 200 g / 7 oz white or brown rice, dry and uncooked

Method

1. Coat the inner compartment of the slow cooker with olive oil or cover it with greaseproof paper.
2. Heat 2 tbsp olive oil in a large frying pan and add the beef or soy mince. Fry over a high heat for 10-12 minutes until evenly browned.
3. Transfer the beef mince or soy mince to the slow cooker.
4. Heat the remaining 1 tbsp olive oil in the frying pan and add the white onion, red pepper, and garlic cloves. Cook for 7-8 minutes until the vegetables begin to soften.
5. Add the chili powder, ground cumin, smoked paprika, dried mixed herbs, salt, and black pepper to the pan. Cook for a further 2 minutes.
6. Stir the tomato puree into the pan and transfer the mixture to the slow cooker. Pour in the chopped tomatoes and mix well.
7. Boil a kettle of water and use it to dissolve the 4 beef stock cubes or vegetable stock cubes if you're making chili non carne. Pour the stock into the slow cooker and stir well.
8. Turn the slow cooker onto a low heat setting and close the lid. Cook the chili for 7 hours.
9. After 7 hours, add the black beans to the slow cooker and continue cooking the chili for another hour.
10. Meanwhile, cook the rice according to the packet instructions. Once cooked, spread the rice evenly across four bowls.
11. When the chili is ready, serve it on top of the beds of rice. Add a side of sour cream and tortilla chips for a delicious dinner.

Chicken and Vegetable Stew

MAKES 4 SERVINGS

PREPARATION TIME – 15 MINUTES

COOKING TIME – 6 HOURS

NUTRITIONAL VALUE PER SERVING – 479 KCALS, 32 G CARBS, 36 G PROTEIN, 23 G FAT

Ingredients

❖ 3 tbsp olive oil

❖ 1 white onion, finely chopped

❖ 1 spring onion, finely chopped

❖ 1 clove garlic, peeled and minced

❖ 2 carrots, sliced

❖ 1 leek, sliced

❖ 2 celery sticks, sliced

❖ 1 x 400 g / 14 oz can of chopped tomatoes

❖ 1 x chicken stock cube or vegetable stock cube

❖ 1 tbsp dried mixed herbs

❖ 1 tsp dried parsley

❖ 400 g / 14 oz skinless, boneless chicken breast, chopped into chunks

Method

1. Coat the inner compartment of the slow cooker with olive oil or cover it with greaseproof paper.
2. Heat 1 tbsp oil in a frying pan and add the onion, spring onion, and garlic cloves. Cook for 7-8 minutes until the vegetables start to soften and become fragrant.
3. Transfer the vegetables to the lined slow cooker compartment.
4. Heat another 1 tbsp olive oil in the pan and add the carrots, leek, and celery sticks. Cook for 7-8 minutes until softened and transfer to the slow cooker.
5. Heat the remaining 1 tbsp olive oil in the frying pan and fry the chicken for 10 minutes until slightly browned. Add to the slow cooker.
6. Pour the chopped tomatoes into the slow cooker.
7. Boil a kettle of water and dissolve the chicken or vegetable stock cube. Add to the slow cooker alongside 1 tbsp of dried mixed herbs and 1 tsp dried parsley.
8. Close the lid of the slow cooker and turn onto a low heat setting. Cook for 8 hours.
9. Serve the chicken and vegetable stew while hot. Store any leftovers in the fridge and consume within 2 days.

Simon Brown

Slow Cooker Pulled BBQ Jackfruit

MAKES 4 SERVINGS

PREPARATION TIME – 10 MINUTES

COOKING TIME – 6 HOURS

NUTRITIONAL VALUE PER SERVING – 214 KCALS, 16 G CARBS, 8 G PROTEIN, 7 G FAT

Ingredients

- ❖ 1 onion, finely sliced
- ❖ 4 tbsp BBQ sauce
- ❖ 2 tbsp BBQ seasoning
- ❖ 1 tsp smoked paprika
- ❖ 1 tsp garlic powder
- ❖ 1 tsp black pepper
- ❖ 400 g / 14 oz jackfruit

Method

1. Coat the inner compartment of the slow cooker with olive oil or cover it with greaseproof paper.
2. In a bowl, mix together the BBQ sauce, BBQ seasoning, smoked paprika, garlic powder, and black pepper.
3. Use a fork to pull the jackfruit into stringy pieces. Add the jackfruit to the bowl and toss to coat.
4. Transfer the jackfruit to the lined slow cooker compartment and close the lid. Turn the slow cooker onto a low heat setting and cook the BBQ jackfruit for 6 hours.
5. Serve the BBQ jackfruit inside a burger bun with a side of chips and salad.

Simon Brown

Slow Cooker Meat-Free Vegetable Lasagne

MAKES 4 SERVINGS

PREPARATION TIME – 15 MINUTES

COOKING TIME – 4 HOURS

NUTRITIONAL VALUE PER SERVING – 654 KCALS, 43G CARBS, 34G PROTEIN, 28G FAT

Ingredients

- ❖ 2 tbsp olive oil
- ❖ 1 white onion, sliced
- ❖ 1 clove garlic, peeled and crushed
- ❖ 2 courgettes, diced
- ❖ 1 carrot, diced
- ❖ 1 red pepper, deseeded and cut into chunks
- ❖ 400 g / 14 oz meat-free chicken style pieces (such as Quorn pieces)
- ❖ 1 x 400 g / 14 oz jar of Alfredo sauce
- ❖ 1 x 400 g / 14 oz can of chopped tomatoes
- ❖ 3 tbsp tomato paste
- ❖ 8 sheets lasagne
- ❖ 50 g / 1.8 oz cheddar cheese, grated

Method

1. Cover the inner compartment of the slow cooker with greaseproof paper.
2. Heat 1 tbsp of olive oil in a large frying pan and add the onion slices and crushed garlic. Cook for 8-10 minutes until they start to soften and become fragrant.
3. Add the courgettes, carrots, and red pepper, and cook for a further 2-3 minutes to slightly soften the vegetables but not fully cook them.
4. Transfer the vegetables to a bowl and set aside.
5. Heat the remaining 1 tbsp olive oil in the frying pan and add the meat-free chicken style pieces. Cook for 8-10 minutes until slightly golden on each side.
6. Transfer the meat-free chicken style pieces to the same bowl as the cooked vegetables.
7. Spread a layer of Alfredo sauce along the bottom of the lined slow cooker tray using a quarter of the total amount of sauce.
8. On top of the Alfredo sauce, spread a quarter of the vegetable and meat-free chicken style pieces mixture.
9. Layer 2 lasagne sheets on top, followed by a third of the can of chopped tomatoes and 1 tbsp tomato paste.
10. Repeat steps 7 to 9 until all of the ingredients have been used. The final layer should comprise 2 lasagne sheets.
11. Close the lid of the slow cooker and turn it onto a low heat setting. Cook for 7 and a half hours.

Simon Brown

12. After 7 and a half hours, open the lid of the slow cooker and sprinkle the grated cheddar cheese on top of the lasagne sheets.

13. Close the slow cooker lid and cook the lasagne for a further 30 minutes to bring the total cooking time to 8 hours. The lasagne should be heated all the way through, the pasta should be cooked, and the cheese should be melted.

14. Serve the lasagne with a side of chips and salad.

Spaghetti and Meatballs

MAKES 4 SERVINGS

PREPARATION TIME – 15 MINUTES

COOKING TIME – 4 HOURS

NUTRITIONAL VALUE PER SERVING – 256 KCALS, 20 G CARBS, 15 G PROTEIN, 17 G FAT

Ingredients

- 1 x 400 g / 14 oz jar of tomato and vegetable pasta sauce
- 400 g /14 oz ground beef
- 2 eggs, beaten
- 1 tbsp soy sauce
- 200 g / 7 oz breadcrumbs
- 1 tsp black pepper
- 1 tsp dried chives
- 4 x 100 g / 3.5 oz nests spaghetti, dry and uncooked
- 1 tsp salt

- 100 g / 3.5 oz cheddar cheese, grated

Simon Brown

Method

1. Coat the inner compartment of the slow cooker with olive oil or cover it with greaseproof paper.
2. Pour the marinara sauce into the lined slow cooker compartment.
3. Place the ground beef in a large bowl and whisk in the eggs and soy sauce.
4. Stir the breadcrumbs, black pepper, and dried chives into the bowl and mix well.
5. Using a spoon or your hands, create small balls of even size until you have used all of the meat mixture.
6. Place the balls into the marinara sauce that is already in the slow cooker. Close the lid and turn the slow cooker onto a high heat setting. Cook the meatballs for 4 hours until the meat is fully cooked and the edges have started to turn crispy.
7. Just before the meatballs are due to finish in the slow cooker, boil a large pan of water. Add the spaghetti and a sprinkle of salt. Cook for 10-12 minutes until the spaghetti has slightly softened.
8. Serve the spaghetti evenly into four bowls and top with the meatball and marinara mixture.
9. Top each bowl with a sprinkle of grated cheese and enjoy!

Desserts and Snacks

When you're craving a sweet treat after dinner or you want a mid-afternoon snack, you'll love all of the recipes that we have got for you to finish up this slow cooker cookbook. Keep reading to learn how to make lots of delicious desserts and snacks.

Slow Cooker Peanut Butter Clusters

MAKES 20 SERVINGS

PREPARATION TIME – 5 MINUTES

COOKING TIME – 2 HOURS

NUTRITIONAL VALUE PER SERVING – 366 KCALS, 28 G CARBS, 9 G PROTEIN, 12 G FAT

Ingredients

◈ 400 g / 14 oz salted, dry roasted peanuts

◈ 100 g / 3.5 oz milk chocolate chips

◈ 100 g / 3.5 oz white chocolate chips

◈ 50 g / 1.8 oz dried cranberries

◈ 50 g / 1.8 oz raisins

◈ 2 tbsp peanut butter powder

◈ 8 tbsp peanut butter

Method

1. Cover the inner compartment of the slow cooker with greaseproof paper.
2. In a large mixing bowl, combine the peanuts, milk chocolate chips, white chocolate chips, dried cranberries, raisins, and peanut butter powder. Use a spoon to stir the ingredients together.
3. Stir in the peanut butter and mix well to fully coat all of the ingredients in the bowl.
4. Spoon the mixture into small, even clusters, and place into the lined slow cooker tray.
5. Close the lid of the slow cooker and turn onto a low heat setting. Cook for 2 hours, checking the make sure that they aren't burning too much after 1.5 hours.
6. Eat the clusters as a snack or for dessert and store any leftovers in the fridge for a maximum of 5 days.

Simon Brown

Strawberry and Coconut Cake

MAKES 8 SERVINGS

PREPARATION TIME – 15 MINUTES

COOKING TIME – 6 HOURS

NUTRITIONAL VALUE PER SERVING – 143 KCALS, 17 G CARBS, 4 G PROTEIN, 12 G FAT

Ingredients

❖ 200 g / 7 oz plain white flour

❖ 1 tsp baking powder

❖ 1 tbsp chia seeds

❖ 200 g / 7 oz fresh strawberries, chopped

❖ 100 g / 3.5 oz coconut flakes

❖ 2 eggs, beaten

❖ 4 tbsp honey

❖ 200 ml milk (any type)
1 tsp vanilla extract

Method

1. Grease a loaf tin with olive oil or butter, or line it with parchment paper.
2. In a bowl, whisk together the plain white flour, baking powder, and chia seeds.
3. Stir in the strawberries and coconut flakes. Add the beaten eggs and honey.
4. Stir in the milk and vanilla extract.
5. Pour the batter into the lined loaf tin and place it in the slow cooker.
6. Shut the lid and turn the machine onto a low heat setting. Cook the cake for 6 hours. Once cooked, the cake should be golden on top. Insert a knife into the centre of the cake and it will come out dry when the cake is ready.
7. Serve immediately or leave to cool on a drying rack. Store any leftovers in an airtight loaf tin for no more than 5 days.

Date, Chia Seed, and Peanut Butter Bites

MAKES 15 SERVINGS

PREPARATION TIME – 10 MINUTES

COOKING TIME – 2 HOURS

NUTRITIONAL VALUE PER SERVING – 178 KCALS, 15 G CARBS, 4 G PROTEIN, 12 G FAT

Ingredients

◈ 400 g / 14 oz pitted dates

◈ 8 tbsp chia seeds

◈ 8 tbsp smooth peanut butter

◈ 100 g / 3.5 oz milk chocolate, broken into pieces

◈ 2 tbsp agave syrup

Method

1. Cover the inner compartment of the slow cooker with greaseproof paper.
2. Place the pitted dates, chia seeds, peanut butter, milk chocolate, and agave syrup in a blender. Pulse in 10-second intervals until the ingredients are well mixed and form a homogenous mixture.
3. Scoop the mixture out in spoonfuls and shape them into even balls.
4. Place the balls into the lined slow cooker tray and close the lid. Cook the date balls for 2 hours on a low heat setting.
5. Remove the balls from the slow cooker and leave them to set in the refrigerator. Store in the fridge for a maximum of 5 days.

Simon Brown

Black Bean Brownies

MAKES 8 SERVINGS

PREPARATION TIME – 15 MINUTES

COOKING TIME – 6 HOURS

NUTRITIONAL VALUE PER SERVING – 189 KCALS, 17 G CARBS, 12 G PROTEIN, 5 G FAT

Ingredients

- 400 g / 14 oz plain flour
- ½ tsp baking powder
- 4 tbsp cocoa powder
- 8 tbsp butter
- 50 g / 1.8 oz milk chocolate, broken into pieces
- 50 g / 1.8 oz dark chocolate, broken into pieces
- 100 g / 3.5 oz granulated sugar
- 400 g / 14 oz dried black beans
- 100 g / 3.5 oz raisins
- 3 eggs, beaten
- 1 tsp vanilla extract
- ½ tsp salt

Method

1. Cover a rectangular brownie tin with greaseproof paper.
2. In a bowl, whisk together the flour, baking powder, and cocoa powder until well-combined.
3. In a large heatproof bowl, place the butter, milk chocolate, and dark. Place the bowl above a pan of simmering water. Warm the mixture over a gentle heat until melted.
4. Remove the bowl from the heat and pour the sugar into the butter and chocolate mixture. Whisk in the eggs, vanilla, and salt.
5. Fold the black beans and raisins into the bowl and mix well.
6. Whisk in the eggs, vanilla, and salt.
7. Stir the flour mixture into the pan until fully combined. Transfer the brownie mixture into a lined brownie tin and place in the slow cooker tray. Even out the top layer of the mixture using the back of a spoon so that it is smooth.
8. Close the lid of the slow cooker and turn it onto a low heat. Cook for 6 hours until the top of the brownie is set, and the inside is hot and gooey.
9. Once cooked, remove the brownie tray from the slow cooker and leave it to cool on a drying rack.
10. Serve the brownie hot or cold with a side of ice cream or whipped cream. Store any leftovers in the fridge for no more than 5 days.

Banana, Caramel, and Walnut Cake

MAKES 8 SERVINGS

PREPARATION TIME – 10 MINUTES

COOKING TIME – 6 HOURS

NUTRITIONAL VALUE PER SERVING – 438 KCALS, 35 G CARBS, 10 G PROTEIN, 29 G FAT

Ingredients

- 1 x 400 g / 14 oz can of condensed milk
- 200 g / 7 oz plain flour
- 100 g / 3.5 oz granulated sugar
- 1 tsp baking powder
- 2 bananas, mashed
- 2 eggs, beaten
- 200 ml cashew milk or oat milk
- 2 tbsp coconut oil
- 1 tsp vanilla extract
- 4 tbsp walnuts, chopped
- 100 ml double cream

Method

1. Remove the label from the can of condensed milk can and place it in a pan. Fill the pan with around 2 inches of water so that the water comes up to around a third of the way up the can.

2. Bring the water to a boil, then lower it to a gentle simmer. Leave the condensed milk to cook for around 3 hours to caramelise the milk.

3. Meanwhile, line a loaf tin with greaseproof paper.

4. In a large mixing bowl, whisk together the flour, granulated sugar, and baking powder.

5. In a separate bowl, combine the mashed bananas, beaten eggs, milk, coconut oil, and vanilla extract.

6. Combine the dry and wet mixtures and mix well until a smooth cake batter forms.

7. Stir the walnuts into the batter, followed by the double cream. Finally, stir in the now-caramelised milk.

8. Carefully pour the cake batter into the lined loaf tin and transfer it into the slow cooker.

9. Turn the slow cooker onto a high heat and cook the cake for 3 hours. When it's ready, it should be set and golden on top. Insert a knife into the middle of the cake and it should come out dry when the cake is ready.

10. Allow the cake to cool on a drying rack before serving. Store any leftovers in an airtight cake tin for a maximum of 5 days.

Vanilla Cheesecake

MAKES 8 SERVINGS

PREPARATION TIME – 15 MINUTES

COOKING TIME – 4 HOURS

NUTRITIONAL VALUE PER SERVING – 222 KCALS, 20 G CARBS, 13 G PROTEIN, 15 G FAT

Ingredients

◈ 400 g / 14 oz digestive biscuits

◈ 4 tbsp butter, melted

◈ 4 tbsp coconut oil

◈ 500 g / 17.6 oz cream cheese

◈ 4 tbsp sour cream

◈ 100 g / 3.5 oz brown sugar

◈ 4 eggs, beaten

◈ 2 tbsp vanilla extract

◈ 1 tsp cinnamon

Method

1. Line a circular cake tin with greaseproof paper.
2. Crumble the digestive biscuits using a food processor or your hands and transfer to a large mixing bowl.
3. Stir the melted butter and coconut oil into the biscuits and mix well so that the biscuit crumbs begin to stick together.
4. Transfer the biscuit crumbs to the lined loaf tin and press down so that the top is smooth and even.
5. In a separate bowl, combine the cream cheese, sour cream, brown sugar, eggs, vanilla extract, and cinnamon. Mix well until all of the ingredients form one, consistent mixture.
6. Pour the mixture on top of the biscuit crumb base. Even out the top of the cheesecake with the back of a spoon.
7. Transfer the cheesecake carefully into the slow cooker. Close the lid of the machine and cook the cheesecake for 6 hours on a low heat setting.
8. Serve the cheesecake while hot or allow it to cool before slicing and eating as a snack or dessert. Store any leftovers in the fridge for a maximum of 5 days.

Simon Brown

Classic Sponge Cake

MAKES 8 SERVINGS

PREPARATION TIME – 10 MINUTES

COOKING TIME – 2 HOURS

NUTRITIONAL VALUE PER SERVING – 256 KCALS, 23 G CARBS, 8 G PROTEIN, 17 G FAT

Ingredients

◈ 400 g / 14 oz self-raising flour

◈ 8 tbsp butter

◈ 2 tbsp olive oil

◈ 200 g / 7 oz caster sugar

◈ 100 g / 3.5 oz granulated sugar

◈ 1 tsp baking powder

◈ 4 eggs, beaten

Method

1. Line a loaf tin with greaseproof paper or grease it with some butter or olive oil.
2. In a bowl, combine the self-raising flour, butter, olive oil, caster sugar, granulated sugar, and baking powder.
3. Whisk in the beaten eggs and stir well to combine.
4. Pour the cake batter into the lined loaf tin. Transfer the tin to the slow cooker and close the lid.
5. Turn the slow cooker onto a high heat setting and cook the cake for 2 hours until golden on top. The cake is cooked when you can insert a knife into the centre, and it comes out dry.
6. Remove the cake from the slow cooker and leave it to cool on a drying rack.
7. Cut into slices and serve with some cream or jam. Store leftovers in an airtight loaf tin and consume within 5 days,
8. Slice into squares and serve up with some jam and whipped cream.

Simon Brown

Slow Cooker Blackberry and Strawberry Cobbler

MAKES 8 SERVINGS

PREPARATION TIME – 15 MINUTES

COOKING TIME – 2 HOURS

NUTRITIONAL VALUE PER SERVING – 278 KCALS, 20 G CARBS, 5 G PROTEIN, 11 G FAT

Ingredients

For the blackberry layer:

- 400 g / 14 oz blackberries, rinsed and drained
- 200 g / 7 oz strawberries, rinsed and drained
- 1 tbsp cornstarch
- 2 tbsp salted butter, melted
- 100 g / 3.5 oz sugar
- For the cobbler layer:
- 400 g / 14 oz cup all-purpose flour
- 50 g / 1.8 oz granulated sugar
- 1 tsp baking powder
- ½ tsp salt
- 300 ml milk
- 1 tsp vanilla extract
- 2 tbsp salted butter, melted

For the topping:

- 1 tbsp granulated sugar
- ¼ tsp cinnamon

Method

1. Cover the inner compartment of the slow cooker with greaseproof paper.
2. Place the rinsed blackberries and strawberries into the lined slow cooker tray.
3. In a bowl, combine the remaining ingredients for the blackberry layer. Sprinkle evenly over the blackberries in the slow cooker.
4. In a bowl, add the all-purpose flour, granulated sugar, baking powder, and salt for the cobbler layer above. Stir in the milk, vanilla extract, and melted butter until well-combined into one smooth mixture.
5. Pour the cobbler batter over the blackberries and use a spatula to even out the top of it.
6. Sprinkle the granulated sugar and cinnamon evenly over the top of the cobbler.
7. Close the lid of the slow cooker and cook the cobbler on a high heat setting for 2 hours until the top layer is hot and golden.
8. Serve the cobbler for dessert, hot or cold, with a side of ice cream or whipped cream.

Slow Cooker Vegan Triple Chocolate Fudge

MAKES 8 SERVINGS

PREPARATION TIME – 10 MINUTES

COOKING TIME – 2 HOURS

NUTRITIONAL VALUE PER SERVING – 344 KCALS, 28 G CARBS, 12 G PROTEIN, 19 G FAT

Ingredients

- ❖ 200 g / 3.5 oz plain flour
- ❖ 100 g 3.5 oz granulated sugar
- ❖ 2 tbsp cocoa powder
- ❖ 1 tsp baking powder
- ❖ ½ tsp salt
- ❖ 200 ml soy milk or oat milk
- ❖ 1 tsp vanilla extract
- ❖ 100 g / 3.5 oz vegan milk chocolate chips
- ❖ 100 g / 3.5 oz vegan white chocolate chips
- ❖ 100 g / 3.5 oz vegan dark chocolate chips

Method

1. Line the inner compartment of the slow cooker with greaseproof paper.
2. In a bowl, add the flour, granulated sugar, cocoa powder, baking powder, and salt. Stir until fully combined.
3. Fold in the soy or oat milk and vanilla extract. Add the milk chocolate chips, white chocolate chips, and dark chocolate chips. Stir well to fully combine.
4. Pour the mixture into the slow cooker and use a spoon to spread the top of the fudge into an even layer.
5. Close the lid on the slow cooker and cook the fudge for 2 hours on low.
6. Leave the fudge to cool on a drying rack and serve hot or cold. Store any leftovers in the fridge for no more than 5 days.

EXCLUSIVE BONUS

40 Weight Loss Recipes

&

14 Days Meal Plan

Scan the QR-Code and receive
the FREE download:

Disclaimer

This book contains opinions and ideas of the author and is meant to teach the reader informative and helpful knowledge while due care should be taken by the user in the application of the information provided. The instructions and strategies are possibly not right for every reader and there is no guarantee that they work for everyone. Using this book and implementing the information/recipes therein contained is explicitly your own responsibility and risk. This work with all its contents, does not guarantee correctness, completion, quality or correctness of the provided information. Misinformation or misprints cannot be completely eliminated.

Printed in Great Britain
by Amazon

11268262R00064